West Kirby
to Hoylake

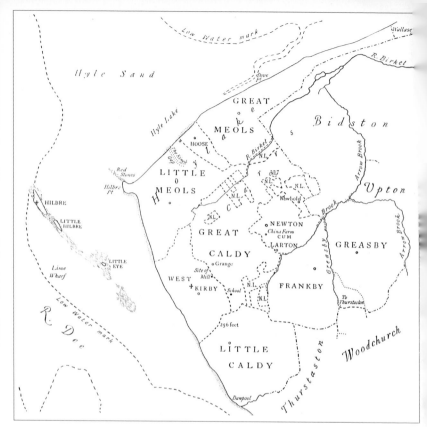

The ancient parish of West Kirby. Hoose is bounded on the west by Lake Place and on the east by Carlton Lane.

IMAGES OF ENGLAND

West Kirby
to Hoylake

Jim O'Neil

NONSUCH

VIEW FROM CALDY HILL, WEST KIRBY.

223283

First published 1994
This new pocket edition 2006
Images unchanged from first edition

Nonsuch Publishing Limited
The Mill, Brimscombe Port,
Stroud, Gloucestershire, GL5 2QG
www.nonsuch-publishing.com

Nonsuch Publishing is an imprint of Tempus Publishing Group

© Jim O'Neil, 1994

The right of Jim O'Neil to be identified as the Author
of this work has been asserted in accordance with the
Copyrights, Designs and Patents Act 1988.

British Library Cataloguing in Publication Data.
A catalogue record for this book is available from the British Library.

ISBN 1-84588-331-4

Typesetting and origination by Nonsuch Publishing Limited
Printed in Great Britain by Oaklands Book Services Limited

Contents

All the advertisements in this book are from *Moss's Directory of Hoylake and West Kirby 1906*, published on 7 December 1905.

Introduction

This book does not attempt to give a full history of the townships in this corner of Wirral; many authors from the Victorian antiquarians to modern writers such as Roberts have compiled very detailed yet readable histories. In choosing the photographs for this collection I was aware that this was not the first book of its kind, and I have tried wherever possible to include items not previously seen.

The area was chosen carefully, with regard to the size of the population and its historical links; most of the places mentioned in this book began as small fishing villages. The increase in mobility provided by the coming of the railways allowed the villages to grow rapidly, and provide homes for those people who could afford to live here and travel into Liverpool. The railways also brought day-trippers and holiday-makers to the beaches and shops in the Victorian and Edwardian eras.

Ironically, it was another step forward in personal mobility – the motor car – that heralded the end of the holiday trade. Resorts such as North Wales, Snowdonia and Blackpool proved more attractive and by the 1950s the holiday boom was over. Today these villages have reverted to their role as dormitory settlements, and the constant stream of traffic past my door has shattered the peace of what used to be a small road of terraced houses and corner shops in the centre of Hoose.

These photographs recall memories of the area as it was until well within living memory – even the last fifteen years have seen vast changes in the fortunes of Hoylake, to an extent which the older residents could never have predicted. Change is a constant process, without which stagnation can set in, but change for its own sake can cause untold loss of the heritage of a town and the local environment; demolition is irreversible. Enjoy this book at your leisure, but learn from it as well, before everything we hold dear is removed to make way for housing estates, superstores, or road 'improvement' schemes.

Jim O'Neil
July 1994

Caldy village cross, from a postcard sent in 1912. The cross is inscribed 'Erected in memory of Alfred Barton of Caldy Manor by many who loved him. Ascension Day 1894'.

One

Caldy

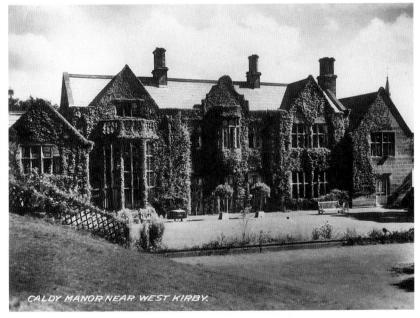

CALDY MANOR NEAR WEST KIRBY.

Caldy Manor, from a postcard mailed in September 1940. The earliest records show that this was originally a small farmhouse, which has since been altered and extended. It was the home of the Barton family for many years and later became the Caldy Heart Hospital. It is now luxury dwellings.

A garden party in Caldy village. The black and white building in the foreground is now two dwellings, 'Corner Cottage' and 'Dee Haven'. This view can only be seen from what is today the steps leading up to the Reading Room, built in 1883, and the costumes suggest a similar date.

Above: Caldy Post Office, from a postcard sent on 17 April 1914. This building has been extended and some alterations have been made to the windows. It is now a private house called 'Tycoed'.

Left: The small Chapel at the Manor was opened in 1882 by Mrs Barton in memory of her husband, Richard Barton, who died in 1881. The Chapel was decorated by C.E. Kempe, who also added the clock turret. This Chapel served the village until the present Church was opened on 1 November 1907, and today it is again part of the Manor House.

Opposite above: Looking north from the centre of the village sometime before 1907, when the Church was dedicated. The black and white building in the centre is the Reading Room, built by the Barton family in 1883. The end gable of the building on the right now has two windows, extremely well matched with the original windows on the far right.

Caldy Village, near West Kirby

Caldy Village, West Kirby

A similar view, but looking in the opposite direction. The Church is visible in the centre, and from the stamp on the back of this postcard this view can be dated to between 1907 and 1918. The Reading Room is on the right, and the building on the left is featured on pages 10 and 11.

13

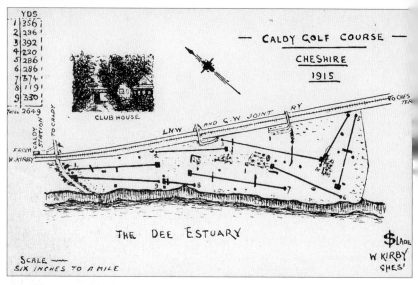

The golf course was laid out in 1908 and extended to 18 holes in 1931.

This postcard was sent on 28 July 1926. Note especially the railway bridge on the left. This clubhouse was sold in 1974.

Caldy Station on a Saturday morning in the early 1950s. The engine is a G.W.R. pannier-back 0-6-0 returning the empties.

The way to West Kirby is via Caldy crossroads, seen here under the control of the old-style traffic policeman, in the days before helmets became compulsory. Note that the rider in the centre has a female passenger.

WEST KIRBY

New Hydro Hotel.

x

Beautifully situated on the Promenade facing the Marine Lake and having fine panorama of Welsh mountains.

Good Boating, Cycling, Tennis, Croquet, Bathing.

NEW BILLIARD AND BALL ROOMS.

Close to the Celebrated Hoylake Golf Links.

BATHS include Turkish, Russian, Electric, Nauheim, Seaweed, Salt Water, Plunge, &c.

Fully Licensed.   Under Entirely New Management.

SPLENDID WINTER CLIMATE, SUNNY AND SHELTERED.

Within easy reach of Liverpool by the Mersey Electric Railway.

Two

West Kirby

THE OLD VILLAGE.

THE BEACH AND PROMENADE.

LOVE TO ALL AT HOME *from* WEST KIRBY

THE PARK.

HOYLAKE HOTEL.

K.5256.

Village Road, in the heart of the old village, early in the twentieth century. In 1905 William Davies was the butcher and the next-door building was occupied by Davis & Son, dyers. Notice the advertising board for the *Courier*. Next to the dyers are 'Tea and Refreshment Rooms. Picnic Parties Supplied'. In the background is the Ring O' Bells public house.

A more hygienic version of the same view – the meat is now inside the shop! On the left is Richard Williams' shop. He combined the trades of grocer, baker, and receiving agent for the Atlas Parcel Express Service. Note the stone under the rear offside wheel of the cart, to stop it rolling backwards.

The bargeboards on the front of the Ring O'Bells proclaim 'RING O'BELLS FAMILY HOTEL', and the present front door is marked 'BILLIARD ROOM'. The Nook, on the left, is built on the sandstone outcrop. This card was mailed on 14 August 1913.

The Ring O'Bells was rebuilt in 1810 on the site of an older building of the same name. The signboard reads, 'Wines and Spirits. Dinners and Teas Supplied. Picnic Parties Catered For. Bait & Livery Stables. Billiards and Bowls'.

The cellars of the Ring O' Bells extend under Village Road, and it is still possible to see where the sandstone bedrock was cut to hold the barrels of ale, with a drainage channel underneath.

The Ring O'Bells Bowling Club enjoys a welcome pint in the early 1960s. Sixth from the right is R.H. Smith, the Club President. Today this area is occupied by a beer garden and an excellent children's playground.

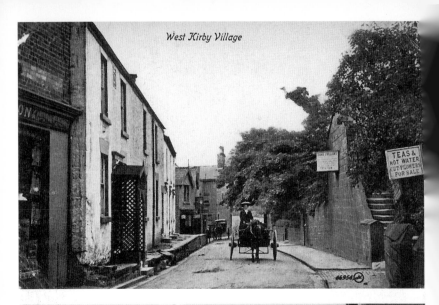

West Kirby Village

Above: St Bridget's Church, photographed by Arthur Goodwin around 1950. There has been a church on this site since about the tenth century, the present building dating from 1870.

Oppostite above: This view is still very much unchanged; note the ubiquitous 'Teas and Hot Water' sign. The other board advertises the services of Frank A. Williams, described in 1905 as 'car proprietor, 14 Alexandra road tel 105'.

Oppostite below: Lower Village decorated for the Coronation in 1953. The car appears to be an Austin A40.

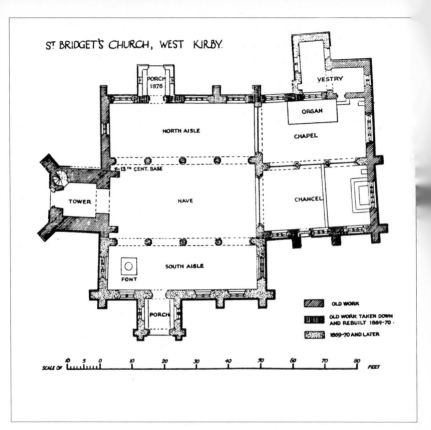

This plan was drawn by Laurence Hobson, F.R.I.B.A., for Brownbill's incredible parish history, printed in 1928.

This postcard was mailed on 4 August 1904, and is remarkable for the sheep grazing in the Rectory Field, presumably to save mowing the grass.

This view probably pre-dates the building of the Marine Lake. Just off to the left of the picture is Dee Lane, with the boats drawn up in much the same position as they would be today. The card was mailed on 10 November 1910.

West Kirby.

The Lake Side.

The Burrovale Series.

This is a very good view of West Kirby but I wouldn't like to walk round the lake I don't like these silly thing. We are all like niggers here. Mary

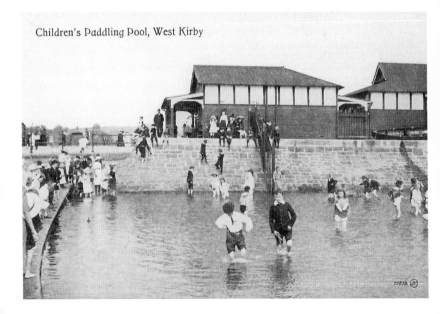

Children's Paddling Pool, West Kirby

75875. (B°)

This postcard will be familiar to many readers, but there is so much detail in it I could not resist the temptation to include it – this one needs a magnifying glass! It appears to have been taken on Sunday 11 May 1954, with a relatively calm sea, at around noon, and in the foreground are the swimming baths. The Hydro, by this time called the Hoylake Hotel, is in the centre, and on the right is the sailing club. Unfortunately, Tell's Tower is just off the right edge!

Opposite above: The Marine Lake at West Kirby was built at a cost of £2,500 and opened on 21 October 1899. This early view of the edge of the lake is postmarked 2 August 1904. The message reads, 'This is a very good view of West Kirby but I wouldn't like to walk around the lake like these silly things. We are like niggers here. [Signed] May'.

Opposite below: A good example of a locally-produced card. It was published by Turners, 4 The Crescent, West Kirby, around the time of the First World War.

The Pool and Promenade, West Kirby   26650

Compare the much more casual costumes in this view, postmarked 30 June 1961, with the photographs opposite.

No trip to the seaside would be complete without a donkey ride, but even the donkeys have to eat! St Peter's Sunday School in Rock Ferry had their Sunday School Treat at West Kirby on 29 July 1914, and someone managed to capture this lovely image for posterity.

Paddle-wheel boats on the Marine Lake in the summer of 1935. The boy in the nearer boat is aged seven, and seems to be wearing his best school uniform!

The summer of 1932, two sisters posing for the family album. Whilst researching this book, more than one person has asked me if these boats existed, or if they have confused memories of one resort with another. They existed.

The West Kirby outdoor baths on a rather windy afternoon, as evidenced by the shadows, waves and flag. Printed in small lettering on the reverse of this card is the uplifting message from the Prime Minister, 'Let us all strive without failing in faith or duty'.

BATHING POOL, WEST KIRBY.   202104. J.V.

A similar view, on a summer's day, with the Hydro Hotel in the background. The card is postmarked 20 August 1933.

The West Kirby Hydropathic Hotel, as it was originally known, was opened in about 1890 and extended in 1896 (see also the advertisement on page 16). In September 1933 the name was changed, as Hoylake was better known nationally through its golf club. Note the ornamental ironwork on the roof.

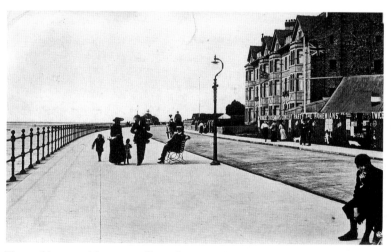

The word 'promenade' was originally a verb, meaning 'to take a walk for pleasure, exercise or show'. The Marine Lake is just visible on the left of this postcard, which was mailed on 27 July 1907. Notice the pavilion on the right, with performances twice daily, admission 1/- (5p) or 6d (2½ p).

Hilbre House, the home of the Macdona family. John Cuming Macdona, M.A., had a varied career. He was born in 1826 and educated at Trinity College, Dublin. He became Rector of Cheadle in 1874 until he resigned in 1882, and became a barrister in 1889. From 1892 to 1906 he was Conservative M.P. for Rotherhithe. He was a celebrated dog-breeder, especially of St. Bernards. He died on 4 May 1907, in London.

Tell's Tower, West Kirby.

John Pride 1939

For biographical details of John Pride, see page 86.

Above and right: This structure is called 'Tell's Tower' and was erected by Cumming Macdona, M.P., in memory of a remarkable Mount St Bernard dog which was buried beneath. A large slab of blue slate can be seen under the Tower, and it bears the following inscription, 'Underneath this Tower lie the remains of Tell, the Champion Rough-Coated Mount St. Bernard Dog of England, and winner of the principal prizes in the kingdom, since his importation by his owner, the Rev. J. Cumming Macdona, in March 1865. He was majestic in appearance, noble in character, affectionate in disposition, and of undaunted courage. Died Jan. 22, 1871. Aged 7 years'.

West Kirby Beach

A group of children pose for a beach photographer in the early years of the twentieth century. Clearly the fashion that season was large hats for the girls, but the sheer amount of clothing that children were expected to wear on the beach was amazing. Note the donkey rides in the background, the side of the cart bearing the name 'Cummings', whose family ran the business for many years. There are also two small dinghies pulled up onto the sand.

Marine Gardens, West Kirby

For the adults, the more genteel pleasures of bowls for the men and mixed doubles at tennis.

An early view of Grange Road. On the left is the railway yard, where the Concourse stands today, and the road on the right is Westbourne Road. The building in the far distance is the White Lion pub. The road rises in the centre to pass over the railway line, now the Wirral Way.

Ashton Park was named after Miss E.M. Ashton who loaned the land in 1899. She died in 1935 and then the Council bought the land. The island in the centre of the lake was a later addition.

A very unusual early view of Grange Road. The building on the right is casting its shadow across the Crescent, on to the large building on the left. This is the Christian Institute, opened on 26 May 1892. It was vested in trustees for undenominational uses, and comprised Reading Room, Lecture Hall with seats for about 350 people and a well-equipped gymnasium. In 1897 the caretaker was Samuel Shore of 5 Stamford Terrace, Tynwald Road. It was in regular use by several organisations, and included a Reading Room and Library for the Y.M.C.A., open from 8.30am to 10.00pm daily. The most interesting feature of this photograph is without doubt the small cottage and the stone wall in front of the building. Comparison with the photographs on the next two pages shows that these must have been demolished soon after the Institute was opened. The Institute itself was demolished in the 1960s and the site is now occupied by the Abbey National Building Society.

A similar view to the photograph on the opposite page. This picture can be dated to between 1897 and 1899 by internal evidence. The sign on the building in the far distance reads 'Grower and Retailer. Flowers and Vegetables', and the Directory shows that in 1905 this was being run by Thomas Totty. The sign on the ground floor of the Institute in this photograph advertises the Bank of Liverpool Ltd, opened in April 1897. In 1905, the Manager was Henry Woolcott, who lived at 9 Lang Lane. The ground floor also housed R. Woolcott & Co., solicitors and commissioners for oaths, part of this company acting as the clerks' office for Calday Grange Grammar School. Over the door of the Bank is a lamp, and there is also a lamp-post outside the Bank. This was probably a gas lamp.

This photograph was taken sometime between 1899 and 1905. The gas-lamp outside the Institute has been replaced by an electric lamp in the middle of the road, the scheme for electric lighting in the area being adopted on 17 July 1899. By the 1920s this lamp had become an obstruction to traffic, and was replaced by a light hanging from overhead cables. The horse-drawn cabs on the left were owned by W.R. Barrington (see the advert on page 6). The small canopy below the station entrance canopy carries the word COAL; the Station Yard included a public weighing machine and ten businesses, at least seven of which sold coal. The Hovis sign on the shops next to the Institute advertises F.C. Hunt, confectioners. The building on the right with the canopy is featured on the next page, and the offices on the extreme right are occupied in this view by A. Harrison, auctioneers. By 1905 it was the surgery of Dr R. Thacker King, and the building was then known as Sandfield House.

Opposite above: This is the canopied building which appears on the right of the last photograph, probably in the early 1900s. Their advertisement in the 1906 *Directory* reads 'PURVEYORS OF MEAT, CORNED BEEF AND PICKLED TONGUES. Families supplied on reasonable terms. It would be esteemed a favour if customers would kindly give their luncheon orders the PREVIOUS DAY'. Today, this building is occupied by Lloyds Bank.

Opposite below: The Crescent, viewed from Banks Road, with the Christian Institute in the background. It is possible to identify some of the shops. On the right of the Institute is Brooks & Co., with one of the few remaining balconies which originally ran all along that side of the road. On the near right corner is Brick Brothers, bootmakers, and the 'hosiers' sign marks Jones & Co., drapers and outfitters. The fashions reflect the prosperity of the area at the turn of the twentieth century.

West Kirby   *Crescent*

The Wrench Series No. 3105

The Public Hall, on the corner of Grange Road and Bridge Road, seen from the corner of Riversdale Road. The Hall was opened on 13 November 1899 and this card was mailed on 5 April 1904. The owners, West Kirby Public Hall and Estate Company Limited, also built a masonic room, a cafe, and a block of twelve shops. The Company Secretary was Mr J.H. Wild.

This interior view of the Hall bears out the advertising claim that it was '... undoubtedly the finest in Wirral and probably in Cheshire'. It could seat 1,200 people '... with ample stage accommodation and every modern convenience'. In 1921 it became the Queens Picture House, which burned to the ground on 28 February 1932. It was rebuilt as the Tudor Cinema and has since had several uses, including a shopping arcade and the local Social Services office. It is currently empty.

Looking down Bridge Road towards Grange Road, around the turn of the twentieth century; the date on the front is 2 November 1903, although it was not mailed until 2 December 1903! On the left is Rutter's Farm.

A closer view of John Rutter's farm in Bridge Road, seen in the picture above.

St Agnes' Roman Catholic Church in Darmond's Green. As late as 1882 there were only three Roman Catholic families in Hoylake and only ONE in West Kirby! From that year visiting priests from Upton or Birkenhead used to say Mass in various temporary rooms. The Church was opened on 18 July 1897, the Presbytery was added in 1903, and the new Sanctuary in June 1905.

This pastoral scene in Darmond's Green has long since given way to the dominance of the internal combustion engine.

John and Mary Rainford on their sixtieth Wedding Anniversary in July 1897. Mary died in 1908 aged ninety-two, and John, a tailor, in 1909, aged ninety-three. It is probable that John had taught himself to read, as he would have been well over school age when the 1870 Education Act was passed.

Dee Cottage in Banks Road. The small lane on the right of the photograph, leading off to the left, is Dee Lane. It is difficult to date the cottage from the known photographs; it is possibly an eighteenth-century building, but the windows appear to be Victorian. It was demolished in July 1936.

This photograph, dating from early in the twentieth century, was taken on land now occupied by the houses in Grammar School Lane. It is possible to see this type of activity today, but only at heritage events and historic sites; it is far too slow and labour-intensive for the modern farmer.

Grange Road, looking towards Meols Drive, with Dee Lane on the left. On the right is the newsagents and tobacconists shop belonging to Frances Ryder, and now owned by Dillons. This block of shops was built in 1899 and cost £15,591.

Essentially the same view, but the Bank of Liverpool, now Barclays, stands on the corner of Dee Lane. They moved from the Institute in February 1908, but the site had been reserved from at least December 1905. The projecting canopy near the bank advertises Hancock's wool shop.

Above: There have been various school buildings at St. Bridget's Church. The foundation stone for the building on the right of this picture was laid on 26 February 1884 by Mrs. Eaton, and opened as a school the following year. This postcard was mailed in 1904.

Left: The sandstone building on the right was known as 'The Old School', and was in use from 1848 to 1864. The schoolroom at Caldy Grange was then used until the building shown above was opened. On 22 November 1892 the Old School was reopened as the Charles Dawson Brown Museum. Brown was well known locally as a local historian, school governor, and 'Friend of the Poor'. He lived at Stone Hive until he died on 4 July 1890. The Museum and its contents has had a chequered history, but it was finally restored and reopened by the Hoylake Historical Society on 24 June 1972.

Above: The Mount, now called Mount Road, on a cold winter day in the 1890s.

Right: The building on the far right of this photograph is in Lang Lane South, and the other two buildings are in Black Horse Hill. The Beacon is visible in the distance.

A magnificent example of a Leyland type 36C7R, one of the first with pneumatic tyres. The fleet number is 165, the registration number is FM3221, indicating that it was registered in Chester, where Crosville had their head office. The sign in the window reads 'MOLD-LOGGERHEADS-RUTHIN-DENBIGH'. The scene is the corner of Riversdale Road and

Grange Road, West Kirby, and the date is 1925, the day the vehicle was delivered from the manufacturers. The conductor is Noel Edwards; the name of the driver is unknown. This vehicle was in service until 1932, when it was sold.

Above: The United Reformed Church, West Kirby. The Church had formerly been Presbyterian. This stands on the opposite side of Bridge Road, here seen on the right, to the Public Hall site. The road on the left is Meols Drive. The Presbyterians began services in West Kirby in 1874, and this, the present building, was opened on 3 April 1890 by the Revd John Munro Gibson, D.D.. The cost including furnishings, was £3,632. It is marvellous to see just how *uncluttered* the scene is in this early photograph; today it is surrounded by a plethora of road signs, yellow lines, pelican crossings, and constant road traffic.

Left: The Revd Patrick Miller Kirkland (1857-1943) was ordained as the Church's first Minister in 1887 and served until his retirement in 1927. He was also instrumental in founding what is now Hoylake-with-Meols United Reformed Church in Greenwood Road, Meols.

The Children's Convalescent Home in Meols Drive, now the Residential School, adjoining the United Reformed Church. The Home started in Filey Terrace, Station Road, Hoylake, moving to the present site in July 1888.

This postcard, sent on 14 July 1929, shows the famous open-air ward, added in 1909 and now fully enclosed.

July 1955, and the 4122 takes on water at West Kirby. The driver on this photograph is Albert Harrison, and the fireman is Alan Hough from Bebington. This locomotive was to go down in history as it pulled the last passenger train to use this line, leaving West Kirby at 2105 hours on Saturday 15 September 1956. In later years it even had a song written about it, especially to remember this event:

> *Four one twenty-two,*
> *The Country Park remembers you.*
> *In every archway you pass through,*
> *You still can hear the whistle of*
> *The four one twenty-two.*

Opposite: Joanna Coath and her horses in Rectory Field, West Kirby, c.1955. Joanna used to run a parcel delivery service from West Kirby Joint Station (always known as 'the Joint'), charging sixpence (two and a half pence) for a trunk, and 4d (1½ p)) for a smaller item. Two railway lines met at West Kirby. The line from Liverpool ran to the present station and is now part of Merseyrail; the other line ran from the Joint Station to Hooton, and is now the Wirral Way. The joint station and the businesses in the station yard were demolished to make room for the Concourse.

This page and opposite: The last lifeboat to be stationed on Hilbre Island was the *Chapman*, a Liverpool-class boat, thirty-five feet by ten feet, built in 1901. She was first stationed at Groomsport in County Down, and in September 1924 she arrived at West Kirby railway station on her way to Hilbre. The crane used was serial number 1483, S.W.L. 5 tons. Notice the plates on the rear wheels of the lifeboat carriage, placed there to prevent them sinking into the sand.

Above: The lifeboat station on this island was built in 1847-8 and was temporarily closed in July 1938. The closure was made permanent on 30 June 1939, and the *Chapman* was withdrawn shortly afterwards. This postcard was mailed on 12 August 1914.

Left: This early photograph of the island clearly shows the Survey Mark, erected in 1912, and also the small cannon in the foreground. This is one of two used until 1890 to signal the Hoylake crew, who could be called to launch either boat. After 1890, rockets were used.

Three

'R.A.F. West Kirby'

R.A.F. West Kirby was started at the beginning of World War II as a training camp, and it later became a transit camp. It stood at the south-west corner of the crossroads in Pump Lane. To be absolutely accurate, 'RAF West Kirby' is something of a misnomer. The camp is in Grange township and the associated housing estate is in Greasby; for many years a daily bus service connected the housing estate with RAF Sealand, near Chester. After the camp closed, almost a whole generation of learner drivers made profitable use of its concrete paths, right-angle turns, and wide visibility. The intention before the War was always to return the land to agricultural use, yet as late as 7 April 1983 local landowners objected to Merseyside Council compulsorily acquiring the 108 acres for this purpose. At that time, much of the site still had roadways, hardstanding, building foundations and drainage manholes. However, the Compulsory Purchase Order was approved on 27 September 1985 and today the site is mainly agricultural once more.

Square-bashing, c.1954.

'The lads from the hut next door ... '

... and their autographs, c.1954.

A team of painters and decorators outside one of the huts, c.1948-50. The author's grandfather, Tommy, is third from left, and the author's father, Reg, is fifth from left, both on the middle row.

A barrack room ready for inspection, c. 1954. Notice the mugs all in perfect precision on the cupboards.

THE

Metaphone

(An Efficient Telephone)

can be fitted to existing
Electric Bell Wires and
will enable you to
immediately telephone
orders to your servants
instead of calling them
into the room, thus
saving their time and
your own.

15/- for the
First Pair
and

7/6

for each
additional
instrument

**Apply to any of the Company's
Offices throughout Great
Britain and Ireland.**

Four

Hoylake

Hoylake consists of two older townships – Little Meolse, today remembered in the name Meols Drive, and Hoose, still the name of the electoral ward and also of a characterless, modern block of flats. Hoose is now the old centre of town. Today, Great Meolse is simply called Meols. In 1792, Sir John Stanley built a hotel to cater for the upper classes partaking of their gentlemanly activities such as shooting, horse-racing, bowls, sea-bathing and, later, golf, but it was the arrival of the railway in 1866 that really caused the three townships to expand as it allowed people to work in the city yet live in the country. The story goes that it was also the railway which caused Meolse to lose its final 'e'. Apparently one of the railway managers was supposed to have copied the spelling from North Meols, near Southport, which was always spelt 'Meols'. Throughout the rest of the book, the modern spelling will be used!

HOYLAKE
STATION 2.

A description of the first railway station at Hoylake states that it was 'an old light-coloured wooden structure', but no photographs have been traced which bear this out. The building on the left of this postcard, mailed on 31 August 1906, is the second station; it was replaced by the existing building in 1938 (see pages 64 and 65). The engine depicted here is locomotive 11.

Opposite above: The nineteenth century Census statistics for the three townships combined are: 1801, 323; 1811, 333; 1821, 404; 1831, 520; 1841, 750; 1851, 929; 1861, 1,017; 1871, 1,576; 1881, 2,536; 1891, 4,076; 1901, 6,352. This graph clearly shows how the railway boosted the rate of population growth in the area.

Opposite below: A composite postcard, probably from the late 1920s or early 1930s, with good quality photographs, but can you spot the mistake? (Answer on page 73).

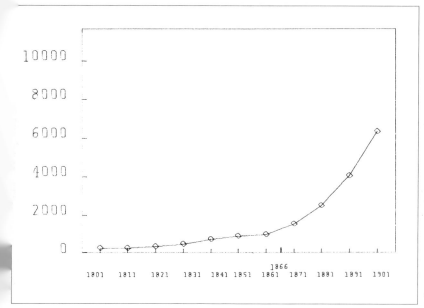

10000
8000
6000
4000
2000
0

1801 1811 1821 1831 1841 1851 1861 1871 1881 1891 1901

1866

THE QUADRANT

COTTAGE HOSPITAL

PROMENADE

HOYLAKE

THE OPEN BATHS

MARKET STREET

The present Hoylake railway station, built in 1938. The architect was possibly influenced by Charles Holden's London Transport stations. It was designed in the Architects' Section of the office of W.K. Wallace, Chief Civil Engineer to the L.M.S. It is now a Listed Building.

This photograph clearly pre-dates British Rail. The "Hornby Dublo" railway sets of the period included stations modelled on this station.

Above: This undated photograph was taken from the footbridge over the line in Station Road. The gasometers have now gone, and the buildings on the right have been replaced by newer workshops, but the overall impression remains much the same.

Left: The Hoylake Urban District Council was formed in 1894, and this was their first crest. The three symbols are, left to right: the Beacon at West Kirby, the Lighthouse at Hoylake, and one of the Dove Marks, which used to be at Dove Point, Meols. This picture is taken from the front cover of the 1897 *Directory*.

This is the second Hoylake crest. The date this was adopted is not known; one possibility is 1932, as the Royden estates at Frankby and Greasby were broken up and sold on 10 August of that year. The Roydens were the last of the old landowners, and from that date Greasby and Frankby became part of the Hoylake Urban District Council area. On 1 April 1974 Wirral Borough Council was formed. 'Respice' means 'looking back' and 'prospice' means looking forward', thus giving the sense of hindsight and foresight. The charges on the shield represent the Wirral peninsula bounded by the two rivers, the Royal Golf Club, the Cheshire wheatsheaf, and various other features of the area.

Above and left: This must be the smallest book of photographs of Hoylake ever made! It is gilt and blue enamel, and would have been fairly expensive for the time. It measures just three-quarters of an inch high and half an inch wide when closed. It contains four sepia photographs of Hoylake and one of Hilbre Island, although originally there would have been a total of six pictures. It dates from *circa* the First World War and books like this were on sale in many holiday towns. The idea was to buy a chain necklace with the first book, and then to build up the collection on successive holidays.

96 Published by F. Ryder,
West Kirby, Photo by A. J. Mart
Hoylake

Fascinating yet frustrating! This picture is captioned 'The Quadrant, Hoylake', but this view is looking away from the Quadrant and may have been taken from the balcony of the Town Hall. Just to the left of Broomfields, the large building in the centre, is a black-and-white gable end. This is the Priory, now Hoylake Jobcentre, which bears the date 1901. The shadows indicate that it was taken mid-morning, and the foliage suggests that it is was summer. But which summer? And what were they all doing? The two cyclists on the corner of Kings Gap are heading towards Market Street, everyone else is going the other way. One of the walkers has a six-pointed 'Jewish' star on his back. Notice also the early 'horseless carriage' just to the right of the centre. Both the photographer and the publisher were local, and it is clear that this was an important event at the time. But what event? And when? This remains a mystery. The postcard was mailed on 29 August 1907.

Golf House & Lin

The Royal Liverpool Golf Club House, pictured early twentieth century. Note the man asleep on the grass! On 13 May 1869 Mr J. Muir Dowie sent out a circular proposing the formation of a golf club at a subscription of 10/- (50p) per year and inviting people to an inaugural meeting two days later. Only seven people attended, yet the plan went ahead and the first match was played on 5 June on a nine-hole course. The golf links occupy the site of the old racecourse, which was in use from 1840 to 8 April 1876, and there was also a small bowling green in the centre of the racetrack. It is not clear just how it was arranged; on the first day of the golf match the press reported that there were some 'amateur horse and pony races', but the novelty of

golf was deemed the more interesting subject. The club became 'Royal' in 1871, when Prince Arthur, Duke of Connaught, accepted the Presidency. Until 1894, when the present clubhouse was built, the club met at the Royal Hotel. In 1911 they bought the freehold of the links from Lord Stanley. In the early years the caddying was done by boys from Hoylake Primary School, sometimes to the extent that the Boys' School was closed for the duration! One entry in the school logbook for 1 July 1903 reads, 'Nine boys allowed from school and their attendances cancelled, to caddy for the Grand Duke Michael of Russia'.

The Quadrant, viewed from Meols Drive. The fence and trees on the right of this picture mark the garden of the thatched cottage shown on the opposite page. The date of this picture can be determined to within a few years; the Quadrant was built around 1900 and the Congregational Church was built on this corner in 1905-6.

Looking south-east across Meols Drive, this thatched cottage stood on the edge of the site of the Congregational Church. The original is, unfortunately, not clear enough to allow us to name the person in the doorway, but he or she was possibly a member of the Roach family. Evidence shows that the photograph was taken between 1884 and 1906.

Opposite below: A detail from a later postcard showing cars and pedestrians at the ornate lamp-post at the top of Kings Gap, known in the area as 'the big lamp' for many years. The present roundabout was constructed in 1937.

Answer from page 62: the top left photograph is incorrectly captioned 'The Quadrant'.

An early engraving, used for the Church Newsletter, which shows the Church as seen from Meols Drive. Note the spire at the west end. The Church became Hoylake United Reformed Church in 1972 and was sold to Hoylake Chapel in 1992.

German World War II incendiary bomb, and top section of a lightning conductor. On the night of 20 December 1940 the Church was hit by a stick of bombs and the spire and the roof timbers were completely burned out. The roof was replaced in 1950 without the spire.

Above: The Sunday School Museum, *c.*1913. This teaching collection was begun in 1911 by the Revd Dr Charles William Budden, who was Sunday School Superintendent from 1904 to 1927. He was well known in Wirral as a Minister, Doctor, and local historian. He lived at 1 Market Street, and reputedly owned the first car in Hoylake.

Right: Twenty-six members of the congregation served in the armed forces during the First World War, and twenty-two of them returned safely. Frank Lester was one of the four who sadly did not return. He was born in Huyton and lived in Irby, but attended this Sunday School and Church, and there is a full memorial to him on the Church wall. He was awarded a posthumous V.C. for courageous action at Neuvilly on 12 October 1918. He was only twenty-two when he died, less than a month before hostilities ceased.

Holy Trinity Church stood in Church Road, later renamed Trinity Road, apparently to save confusion with Church Road, West Kirby. The land was donated by Betty Swainson, widow of John Timothy Swainson, and the foundation stone was laid on Monday 9 April 1832. It was designed by Picton, the famous Liverpool architect, was consecrated on 1 November 1833 and became the Parish Church of Hoylake in 1860.

Hoylake Parish Church

John Pride 1939

For biographical details of John Pride, see page 86.

An early picture of St. Hildeburgh's Church (note the spelling mistake!), taken when it was only two or three years old. Note also the hosepipe in the foreground.

Originally built as a Chapel of Ease, St. Hildeburgh's Church in Stanley Road was designed by Edmund Kirby, also a Liverpool architect. Construction was begun in September 1897 and, although not quite completed, it was opened for worship on 1 May 1899. It was consecrated on 7 September 1899 and became the Parish Church of Hoylake in 1976, when Holy Trinity Church was demolished. The building in the background is now the King's Gap Court Hotel.

Building of the Town Hall began in February 1897 and it was opened on 2 February 1898, by Colonel E.T. Cotton Jodrell, M.P. The following description is taken from the *Herald and Visitor*, the forerunner of the *Hoylake News*, on 27 March 1897: 'These buildings are now in course of erection on a site at the junction of Market Street with Albert Road, Hoylake, from the designs of Mr. Thomas W. Cubbon, Architect, of Birkenhead, who obtained first premium in our open competition. The entrance to Public Offices is from Market Street, to the right of which the Town Clerk's, Medical Officer's Department, and Council Chamber are arranged, the Surveyor's and Rate Collector's Departments being on the left. The Fire Station fronts Albert Road, and consists of engine house, assembly room and large yard. The remaining portion of ground floor is arranged for technical classes, &c. The first floor consists mainly of

large Public Hall, capable of accommodating about 500 people, three entrances being provided, one from Market Street and two from Albert Road. Ladies' and gentlemen's dressing rooms and large refreshment room are arranged in connection with Hall. The Caretaker's House is over the Fire Station and is approached from Albert Road. The buildings will be faced with red Ruabon bricks with dressings of Runcorn stone and terra cotta. The Fire Station and Technical block have been carried out by Messrs. Hill & Co., of Woolton, Liverpool, and a tender for Public Offices and Hall, submitted by W.H. Forde of Birkenhead, has been accepted. The total cost of Buildings will be about £5,000'. As I wrote in 1994, the Town Hall stood empty and forlorn, the most prominent feature being the 'For Sale' signs. Since then it has been restored to an extremely high standard as "Hoylake Jobcentreplus."

A view beloved of photographers for over a century, but I make no apologies for including it as I consider it the best I have seen. The detail is excellent; I particularly like the postcards on sale under the arcading (all demolished now, except in front of one shop), the handlebars on the bicycle on the far right and the lady lifting her skirt to avoid the piles of horse-droppings

all along the road! On the rear of the horse-drawn van can be seen an advertisement for 'Harry Eccles & Co., The Stores, Hoylake'. In 1905 this company had shops at 42 Market Street and 18 Birkenhead Road. The van also mentions that they were 'Tea, Coffee & Provision Dealers' and 'Importers of Finest Irish Butters'.

Above: J. Haskins & Sons had two shops, this one at 76 Market Street, where Lo-Cost stands today, and one in Grange Road, West Kirby. In 1905 the firm was described as 'golf club and ball makers, hairdressers and tobacconists'. In this photograph, taken c.1920s, 'Pop' Haskins stands on the left, and on the right is George Whiteley, Pop's son-in-law.

Market Str., Hoylake

Above: This card was posted on 2 August 1911, although it is difficult to say when it was taken. Let us assume that the boy on roller skates was not playing truant. It appears that the bank in the centre of the photograph had its door open; the shadows indicate early afternoon, and the foliage suggests early spring. We know from the directories that at the time all the banks closed at 12.30pm on a Saturday, so this could be around that time, although the date remains obscure.

Right: This dapper gentleman is striding past the corner of Melrose Avenue, formerly Cross Street, the wall on the right belonging to the Ship Inn, seen in the next photograph. The butcher's shop behind him has long gone; for many years it was Rumbelows, and now it is a charity shop. Records show that the first building to occupy that corner site was a butchers.

At first glance this photograph, taken about 1900, is easily recognisable as the Ship Inn, but closer study reveals that there have been major changes, and in fact only the three chimney-stacks and the bay window remains unaltered. The *Directory* of 1897 gives John Richards as the landlord, but by the time the 1901 edition was published the pub was in the hands of his executors. In 1905 the landlord was W.H. Poingdestre, and it then passed through various licensees including the Croft, Broster and House families.

Opposite above: This photograph dates from around the 1920s, the man on the right is Rex Wilson. According to *Hawling's Directory*, 1922 edition, T.M. Stephenson & Son were at 20 Market Street, now occupied by Broster's delicatessen.

Opposite below: This postcard was mailed on 19 September 1908. The road on the right is Shaw Street. The blocks of shops on that side of the street are mainly unchanged, but the other side is virtually unrecognisable.

O HOYLAKE

This photograph, from around the turn of the twentieth century, shows a block of cottages which stood on Market Street. They were demolished to make way for the Kingsway Cinema, which opened on 10 July 1915 and closed on 12 March 1960. It was then demolished and the site is now occupied by Kwik-Save and the adjoining shops.

Oppostite above: John Foster Pride was born in Liverpool in 1877, and spent many holidays in Parkgate when a boy. He loved the Wirral and drew pictures and wrote poems about the countryside. He had tuberculosis, and spent 1937-38 in hospital. He then lived in Heswall until he died in March 1941.

Opposite below: Perhaps this card could be re-named 'Hoylake Old and Even Older.' Some of the buildings are recognisable; the shop on the extreme right is now the fishmongers, and in the far distance can be seen the arched front of what is now the Wirral Horn Arcade, with the roof of the former sub-Post Office behind.

Home Farm, The Goose Common, Meols.

John Pride
1930

Hoylake
Old & New
John Pride

This aerial view of Hoose was taken in the summer of 1981, but the scene could have been taken twenty years earlier. The large building just to the right of centre is the Parish Hall.

The opening of the Parish Hall in Grove Road, *c.*1929-31. Early in August 1977, whilst in the final stages of reconstruction, the Hall was burned to the ground during the night, causing £100,000 worth of damage. The Hoylake C.I.D. suspected arson. It was rebuilt and used for several years, but has recently been demolished and replaced by houses.

Opposite: Another well-known local figure, Herbert Doyle, from Grange View, on Meols Drive.

Above and below: The officers and some of the men of the 433rd Battery, 149th Regiment, Royal Horse Artillery at Hoylake, on 17 September 1939. There are apparently two different 'originals'

of this photograph; the one I was loaned is thirty inches long by six inches high, and that's the 'short' version!

Returning to Market Street, Shaw Street is on the left by the man with the handcart, from a photograph taken during the 1920s. The large building with the projecting sign is the Punchbowl public house, the second of that name. The first Punchbowl was a small thatched cottage with little accommodation, at least until the stables at the front facing the main road were converted to make more space. In mid-Victorian times it was the only place to go to hear someone read the newspaper aloud. The landlord was John Shaw. The cottage was later replaced by this building, which narrowed the road and formed a bottleneck; schoolchildren used to love to lean out of the top of the bus and try to grab a branch from the large tree as they passed the pub! It was acknowledged as early as 1918 that there was a traffic problem, but it was not until 1936 that the present building, in an older style, was constructed.

A. LILWALL,

THE VICTORIA MILLS, RUDD STREET,

Telephone 20 Y. **HOYLAKE.**

DEALER IN

Hay, Clover, Straw, Bran, Chop, &c.

Special Value in Poultry and Pigeon Corn

Everything for the feeding of Horses, Cattle and Poultry, at wholesale prices.

Crushing and Grinding for Farmers.

Free Deliveries Daily Throughout the District.

OUT-DOOR PHOTOGRAPHY

Houses, Groups, &c., photographed on the shortest notice.

Portraits taken either Day or Night in the Studio by Electric Light.

Limelight Lantern for Lectures and Children's Parties

For Terms apply to

A. J. MARTYN,

4 Central Hall Buildings, Albert Road, Hoylake.

This beautiful thatched cottage, probably built in the late eighteenth or early nineteenth century, belonged to the Barlow family. It can be clearly identified on the First Edition of the 25" O.S. Plan, surveyed in 1871. However, by the time the Second Edition was published in 1897, it had been demolished to make way for Wood Street. Today, the D.I.Y. shop would be on the

photographer's left, and the Trustee Savings Bank on his right. It was originally intended to use the name Barlow Street, which would have had some meaning, rather than Wood Street, which would not, since there were no trees in the area. However, it was named Wood Street by an owner of one of the adjacent properties, who also owned premises in Wood Street in Liverpool.

The first school in Hoose was built in School Lane in 1836, and was later extended to about four times its original size. It has recently been demolished, and a block of flats built on the site. The Market Street building, now standing empty, opened on 4 August 1891, the present building on 2 November 1978, and the Junior Extension on 7 December 1989. The first headmaster was Stephen Stanley; he met his wife, Eliza (née Teeton), during their training at Chester College. Stephen died on 29 March 1869 aged just thirty-three, and is buried in the churchyard in Trinity Road. These photographs were reproduced from daguerreotypes dating from around 1860. These are glass negatives treated to a appear positive.

This is the oldest-known class photograph for the area, taken in the Market Street building in 1904.

In 1928, at the age of 14, Fred Clarke was presented with no less than an engraved gold watch for ten years' perfect attendance. The photograph shows Revd Canon W.T. Warburton, M.A., Vicar of Hoylake and Chairman of the Managers, presenting the watch. Mr Robert Dun, another school manager and honorary correspondent for the local press, is on the left.

Class 3, Holy Trinity School, Hoylake, 1953. This is one of the last group photographs to include the headmaster, John Molyneux ,on the left, as he retired that year. The teacher on the right is Mr Jones. On the top row, second from left, is Laurie Gartside, and the boy in the centre wearing the medal is Raymond Waite, who was a newsagent in Hoylake for many years.

There have been two lighthouses at Hoylake since as early as 1764, to guide ships through the treacherous sandbanks and shifting channels around the north Wirral coast and into Liverpool. This is the Upper Lighthouse in Valentia Road, photographed early in the twentieth century. It was built in 1865 and last lit on 14 May 1886. It has nineteen obvious rooms, but behind the mirrors and curtains are hidden rooms and a maze of secret passages.

The Lower Lighthouse at the bottom of Alderley Road was identical, except that it was not as tall. It was also built in 1865, and was last lit on 14 July 1908 (although some sources state 1 July). It then became the entrance to the Lighthouse Pavilion Theatre, which hosted variety acts and later became a cinema, now one of the handful that survive in Wirral. However, the lighthouse was not so fortunate, being demolished in December 1922. Note the water pump in the yard.

There have been three lifeboat houses at Hoylake; no photographs appear to exist of the first one and all we know about it is that it was built of wood in September 1803. This is the second, built on the same site. Note the fishing fleet at anchor – today Hoylake has just two fishermen – and the lifeboat carriage with the large wheels in the centre. The Lower Lighthouse is on the right, and the bench seat is next to one of several early attempts at coastal defence. In 1898 Hoylake Urban District Council started planning the promenade, which meant that this building had to be demolished. The deal struck in June of that year was that the R.N.L.I., who had owned this building since 1894, would move out. The Hoylake Urban District Council would give £200 towards a new building, and also build the slipway, and the M.D. & H.B. would grant the site for the new (present) building. This was completed in 1899, at a cost of £922.

Although the caption to this postcard reads 'Launching the Lifeboat, Hoylake', it seems clear that the boat was not moving when photographed; there is no-one on board and the weather appears fine. Possibly it was out on public view, or for maintenance. The card was mailed on 16 July 1913, but the picture was clearly taken earlier as the boat is the Coard William Squarey, in use from 1894 until 1904. Note the outsize wheels on the carriage, to prevent it sinking into the sand.

Thomas Dodd (1860-1916) seen here on Hoylake beach in winter 1897. He was appointed Coxwain of the Hoylake Lifeboat in July 1894. On 16 October 1902 in a howling gale, Thomas managed to get the lifeboat aside the stricken Russian barquentine *Matador* and rescue the nine-man crew. For his bravery that night he was presented with the R.N.L.I. Silver Medal on 13 December, and later the crew each received certificates from the Imperial Russian Association for Life-Saving. Could this really be the same Thomas Dodd who, in his first year at Hoose Junior Boys School, was 'cautioned ... against pricking his donkey with pins'? Thomas filled the post of Coxwain until his death in January 1916.

Above: The opposite corner of Alderley Road from the cinema, with Hilbre Island in the background. This card was published in Wallasey, probably in the 1950s. The site is now occupied by a block of flats.

Right: The Lighthouse Pavilion was built between October 1910 and August 1911, and in Summer 1920 it was renamed the Pavilion Super Cinema, which dates this photograph to within ten years. It is advertising 'Concerts Daily at 3.15 and 6', although there was sometimes a later show, usually at 8.00pm.

This photograph dates from early in the twentieth century, and is simply captioned 'Children's Corner'. It is frustrating that, it does not give any indication of what is happening. The large building, left of centre, is Fellowship House, at the bottom of Trinity Road, then called Church Road.

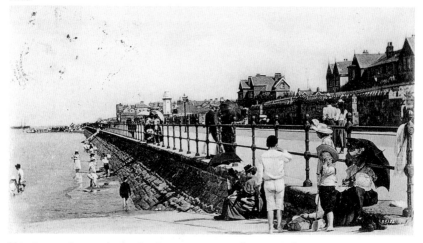

This picture at least can be dated with some accuracy, as the promenade was completed in Spring 1899 and the card is postmarked 17 July 1905. The Lower Lighthouse marks the bottom of Alderley Road.

This view probably pre-dates the First World War, as it was mailed on 24 July 1915 – I wonder how many of these men survived? Note the three-wheeled bathchair, right of centre, and the small jetty in the distance, which still appears on some maps although it vanished about thirty years ago.

PROMENADE AND BATHS, HOYLAKE.

G2366

Hoylake Baths from a postcard mailed on 11 July 1947. It is interesting because it shows that two-way traffic was possible along that part of the promenade.

H 593 The Beach showing Ellen Conner

This postcard is full of interesting details. It was published in Hoylake by The Handy Stores at 72 Market Street, and is postmarked 5 September 1929. The message on the back, from Ada to Uncle Joe, is typical of the period. It concludes, 'We have been sailing and went a chara. drive last night'. The sign on the main building simply reads 'Girls Hostel'; by 1923 the Ellen Gonner Home had room for seventy children. The horse-drawn van on the right advertises 'Patrick's Ices – Guaranteed Pure!'. The scene on the beach is reminiscent of seaside holidays everywhere; note

ome. Hoylake

the piles of deckchairs for hire. The shadows suggest midday, and the canvases on the deckchairs
show that it was breezy. The lady with the reading book has her coat fastened, so it was probably
not very warm – perhaps it was early in the season? On the left of the picture are the sandhills,
later to be covered by a housing estate, and the toilet block by the slipways has yet to appear.
The lookout and flagpole have since vanished.

An artist's impression of the planned Hoylake Institute, from a postcard mailed on 19 December 1903. The comment on the bottom, which is dated 12 December 1903, reads, 'Total takings for three days £603 – this is good work – & we hope to clear £550 for the Institute. It has been hard work all through'. The Hoylake Temperance Society was formed at Hoylake Presbyterian Church in 1882, and they were responsible for the building of the Institute. The foundation stone was laid by Lord and Lady Stanley of Alderley on 20 July 1904. The building was of Ruabon bricks, with stone facings and Welsh slates. The cost, including furniture, was about £6,000. The premises were opened on 16 December 1904 by the Mayor of Liverpool.

In October 1912 Messrs. George Fenton and Victor Branford leased the Institute for use as a cinema until at least July 1915, some sources stating 1919. The building was taken over by the Y.M.C.A. in 1921, and in 1936-7 the basketball team were All-England Champions and represented England at the Paris Exposition in 1937. Apart from the section on the left of the photograph, which is now Hoylake Evangelical Church, the building was demolished in 1986 and a fund was set up to raise money for a commemorative stone. (At that time the author had a shop in Hoylake, and put on a window display in support). The plaque was erected outside Elmtree Court, which now occupies most of the site, on 30 October 1987.

This picture can be dated to sometime between 1904, when the Institute was built (just visible on the left), and 1910, when the Cottage Hospital was erected – in this photograph the site is still sandhills. The workman on the left has unconsciously struck the pose of workmen everywhere – leaning on his shovel! In the foreground Chapel Road is on the left, with Hoyle Road on the left in the middle distance. The block of shops on the right runs between Lee Road and Newton Road, but the gable end in the middle distance on the right is Manor Road; the block of shops which now stands between Newton Road and Manor Road had not yet been built. Notice the wonderful telegraph poles, which even had decorative finials on the top.

Opposite above: This photograph is a little later than the view opposite, and is taken from a postcard mailed on 15 August 1911. The block of shops missing from the last photograph is seen on the right, with a group of people outside the shop now occupied by George Crowder Associates. There is still not Cottage Hospital in sight, however, so we can date this view to 1905-9. Manor Road is on the right.

Opposite below: With the growth in population at the end of the nineteenth century, pressure grew for local medical facilities so that travelling to hospitals in Liverpool or Birkenhead could be avoided. The first District Nurse for Hoylake was appointed in 1899 and in 1906 a temporary hospital was opened in a rented house in Church Road, now Trinity Road, with six beds. The Cottage Hospital was opened in 1910 with ten beds and it was extended in 1927. It then had twenty-eight permanent and eight temporary beds, with sunrooms and verandahs. Although it was closed by the Health Authority in 1983, the Cottage Hospital is one of Hoylake's success stories. It has been reopened by the H.C.H. Trust and recently extended again, and facilities such as a minibus have been provided. This plan was surveyed in 1954, and revised in 1970.

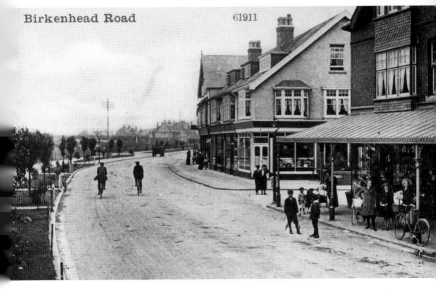

Birkenhead Road 61911

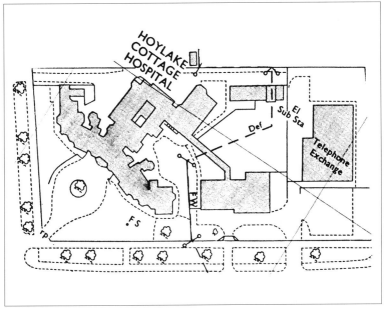

HOYLAKE COTTAGE HOSPITAL

Walker's Tea Rooms at 28 Government Road. The Tea Rooms were built in 1878, but I cannot find any mention of the business in any of the directories of the period. This was the meeting place of the Hoylake Cycling Club, pictured on these two pages, in the early years of the twentieth century. The man in the lead appears to have a false right hand. The intertwined H.C.C. monogram can be seen under the projecting sign by the window, but again there seems to be little information available about the Club.

Four young ladies on the steps of the tea rooms.

Heading up Thurstaston Hill in 1903 – no worries about single file in those days!

Cycling along the promenade from Hoylake to Meols in 1903. The man from third from left is Bill Flanagan.

Birkenhead Road has brought us to Meols – formerly Great Meolse – and in great style! This traction engine was apparently built by Bridson's of Neston, from parts of at least three engines. Mr. Bridson is on the left.

114

Five

Meols

A job well done! On the far left is Ronnie Capper of the well-known local firm Tottey & Capper.

The lettering at the top reads, 'Minshall Bros. & Foxhall. Automotive Engineers, Bridgnorth, Salop'. The scene is somewhere in the Dovepoint Road area.

The early history of Meols lies buried under the sand and the waves. Some 6,000 years ago the area was forested, and in Victorian times the remains of tree-trunks were often exposed at low tide. As recently as 1982 the peat beds in which these trees grew were visible. In Roman times there was some sort of trading post here, connected with Chester by sea and road, and hundreds of Roman and Medieval coins were found and recorded in the 1860s. The coastal erosion in this area is tremendous; measurements taken between 1895 and 1900 show that the coast had moved back no less than eighty-eight feet in that time. In other words, if the modern sea defences had not been built, Market Street would have ceased to exist in 1954!

This view, probably taken in the 1940s, suggests that the water and the slipways were very much cleaner than they are today. By the time this postcard was sent, on 21 August 1950, tourism in the area was in decline.

Meols School was opened on Monday 11 October 1880 in School Lane, Meols, as the existing school in School Lane, Hoose, was becoming overcrowded. This photograph was taken in the late 1890s or early 1900s. Third from right, on the front row, is Rex Wilson. The Headmistress at that time was a Mrs Salt.

This group of men dressed as minstrels was taken on the promenade at Meols early in the twentieth century. Looking from left to right the first two are Bill Flanagan (who is also pictured on page 113) and Bob Eccles.

The boy in this picture is standing at the corner of Forest Road. On the right is Rose Cottage, with Shaws Drive on the extreme right. The large building on the left is now 140 and 138 Birkenhead Road. Probably the most interesting thing about this photograph of The Goose Green, Meols, is the pile of what looks like kerbstones on the grass. I suspect that these indicate that construction was about to start on Roman Road. The Minutes of the General Purposes Committee of the Hoylake Urban District Council record that on 14 October 1901 they decided on the names for the new roads forming the Meols Improvement Scheme: Forest Road, Roman Road, Deneshey Road, Hoyle Road, and Chapel Road. As this view shows Forest Road to be at least partly built, and Roman Road just being started, it must date from 1900 or 1901.

Resting in the sunshine, after a 'spiffing game of croquet' on the front lawn. The Elms in Park Road, probably in the late 1920s.

The gable end on the right is 15 School Lane, and a modern bungalow called The Crofton now stands on the corner of Brosters Lane on the left. Most of the trees in this view have gone, as have the houses in the far distance, but the walls and gateways of Hawthorn Terrace remain unchanged. Note the man and young child on the right. This card was mailed on 5 July 1913.

This card is from the same series as the one above, both published in Liverpool, but it is not possible to identify the buildings shown and the card was never mailed.

An excellent early view of Forest Road, with Birkenhead Road behind the photographer, and the corner of School Lane on the right. Sloop Cottage is on the left; in the 1841 Census this was listed as The Sloop Inn, John Cookson being the licensee. In this picture it is simply advertising 'TEAS and hot water'.

White Cottage among the sandhills on a very windy day early in the twentieth century. Forest Close now occupies this area.

An early view of the pond at Meols, adjoining the railway station. The road bridge over the line can be seen in the middle distance.

There is a story that Braithwaite Poole, the General Manager of the railway, created the pond deliberately to attract anglers in the summer and ice skaters in the winter, who would travel by train and thereby increase the railway's profits!

While engaged in the research for this book I came across a copy of the 1987 reprint of *Contemporary Biographies – Cheshire*, first published in 1904. This contains biographies of 612 Cheshire gentlemen, of which nine were dead. There were, of course, no women. Out of the total, just the four pictured on these pages (less than one per cent) were from this area. The details given here are based on the 1904 text.

BLENCOWE. Reverend Canon Alfred James Blencowe, M.A., St Bridgets Rectory, West Kirby. Blencowe was born in Northamptonshire in 1848, and went to Oxford University. He was ordained in 1874 and later worked for four years at Chester Cathedral. He became Rector of West Kirby in 1889.

CHRISTIAN. William Watson Christian, Ronaldsway, West Kirby. Christian was born in the Isle of Man on Christmas Day, 1842. He settled in Cheshire in 1864 and was very active in promoting the development of Hoylake and West Kirby for many years.

RANKINE. Adam George Rankine, J.P., Redcroft, Hoylake. Rankine was a Scot, born in Ayrshire in 1852, and educated at Edinburgh Academy. He was a cotton merchant in Liverpool until his retirement in 1901. In 1902 he became Captain of the Royal Liverpool Golf Club.

ROYDEN. Thomas Bland Royden, D.L., J.P., Frankby Hall. The Roydens were ship-owners, and Thomas was also very active in politics both in Liverpool and nationally. He was Chairman of the training ship *H.M.S. Conway.*

The Reliance Teeth Manufacturing Company factory at 13 Celtic Road, Meols. This view was probably taken from the rear of 40 Park Way. On the left is the rear of 18 Cranborne Avenue, the gables on the right being numbers 24 and 26. The business was founded in 1905 in Liverpool by Robert Grave, Gilbert Rigby and Esmond Rigby. The Company moved to Meols in 1908 when this factory was built, and at one time they also had subsidiary premises in Trinity Road, Hoylake. Up to the Second World War they produced porcelain teeth, but then plastic teeth were invented and Reliance made both types. However, the manufacture of plastic teeth needed less labour and the workforce dropped from sixty to just twenty-five in 1971, at which time it was the only industry in Meols. The factory closed down at the beginning of July 1971. The site was sold, and it is now covered by houses.

Vickers VA-3 Hovercraft, fitted with four Bristol Siddeley Turmo 603 turbines. Yes, I know this is not Hoylake, but it was planned to be there! The world's first passenger hovercraft service operated between Moreton and Rhyl from 20 July to 16 September 1962. The original plan, however, was to run from Hoylake, but on trials it became obvious that the engines were much noisier than had been realised, which sparked off a great debate. Hoylake Council, who thought that they were living up to the 'foresight' part of their motto by agreeing to the service, called a public meeting at the end of May 1962. It became clear that ninety-five per cent of the residents were in favour of the service, but the other five per cent strongly opposed it; apparently not because of the noise, but because Hoylake might be exposed to a flood of visitors. Not only does this incident show that the tourist boom in Hoylake was at an end, but most of all, it demonstrates that a vociferous minority wanted it that way (although I am left wondering what the shopkeepers thought at the time). The companies involved reluctantly agreed to find another beach, settling on Moreton in the end.

Acknowledgements

Compiling a volume such as this is impossible without the interest and generosity of many people. Some wished to remain anonymous; in alphabetical order the others are as follows – with apologies to anyone I have accidentally omitted:

Mr Armitt, Bernard Barlow, Vic Bradley, Norman Broster, Mrs Clothier, Joanna Coath, John Cook, Mrs Formstone, Laurie Gartside, Martin Green, Edna House, Mrs McCready, Mrs McGinn, Cath Masterson, Rose Meldrum, Ann Neilands, Jim Peden, Eric Power, John Ryan, Mr Simons, Mrs Smith, Mrs Waring, Eric Wilson, Mrs Wood, D & M Young.

I would also like to thank all the Wirral libraries, the *Wirral News*, the *Wirral Globe*, the *Liverpool Daily Post* and Claire Bowles and the staff of Radio Merseyside for the publicity and historical information they have supplied.

Last but not least, I must thank David Buxton and all his staff at Alan Sutton Ltd for their help and patience.